Amazing Ants

by Margie Sigman   illustrated by Peter Church

Harcourt

Orlando Boston Dallas Chicago San Diego

Visit *The Learning Site!*

www.harcourtschool.com

Printed in China

ISBN 0-15-325488-2

12 13 14 15 16 17 18 19 20 121 10 09 08 07 06 05

Ordering Options
ISBN 0-15-325468-8 (Collection)
ISBN 0-15-326566-3 (package of 5)

Ants can smell.
They can smell the red grapes.

Ants can walk.
They can walk in a long line.

Ants can cut. They cut
the grapes into little bits.

Ants can lift.
They lift up the grapes.

Ants can walk.
They walk back to the hill.

Ants can climb.
They climb down into the hill.

Ants can eat!